Floral Nature Embroidery Designs

De-ann Black

Text copyright © 2017 by De-ann Black
Cover Design & Illustrations © 2017 by De-ann Black

Published 2017

ISBN: 978-1975629175

This book has over 50 floral and nature theme embroidery designs. The designs include: lily of the valley, fuchsia, sweet peas, chocolate daisies, bluebells, lavender, violets and all sorts of other flowers, along with bees, butterflies, birds, moths, ladybugs, seahorse, squirrel, owl and dragonflies as well as little tea cups, teapots and cupcakes.

De-ann Black is the designer and illustrator. The motifs are created from her original artwork.

The book contains full-size templates on single-sided pages so you can trace or transfer the designs on to fabric ready for embroidering.

The designs are ideal for hand stitching and hoop embroidery. Many of the motifs fit into standard size 7 inch, 6 inch, 5 inch and 4 inch hoops.

Lots of the main designs have smaller/larger size versions included, along with other little motifs suitable for stitching.

Please note: This is a book of embroidery designs only (motifs, templates). It does not contain sewing or stitching instructions. Just the designs. Please take a peek inside the book using the look inside feature to see a sample of the contents.

You can choose your favourite stitches and threads to sew the designs. Pictures of some of the items are shown on the cover of the book. These were stitched by De-ann to show how some of these designs look when embroidered.

De-ann Black Website: De-annBlack.com

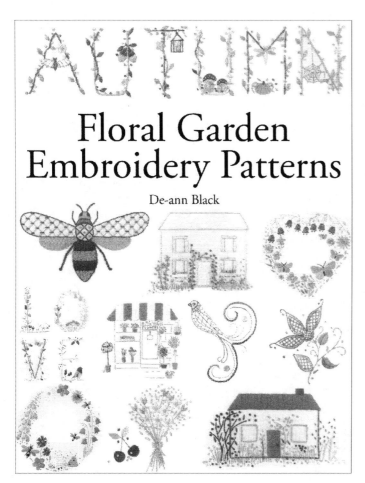

De-ann's new embroidery book Floral Garden Embroidery Patterns is out now.

The book has over 100 floral and garden theme embroidery patterns. The patterns include: a floral garden cottage, an autumn cottage, bee gardens, bluebells, forget-me-nots, lily of the valley, autumn garland, winter garland, Christmas roses, strawberry flowers, bramble bee designs, cherry blossom flowers, birds, bees, butterflies, ladybirds, dragonflies, toadstools, acorns, floral arch, a flower well, beehives, flower baskets, pretty bouquets, a flower shop — and lettering patterns for the words Spring, Summer, Autumn, Winter, Daisy and Love.

Most of the patterns use stranded cotton embroidery thread (floss), but crewelwork patterns (wool embroidery) are included. The crewel wool patterns can also be stitched with cotton embroidery thread if preferred.

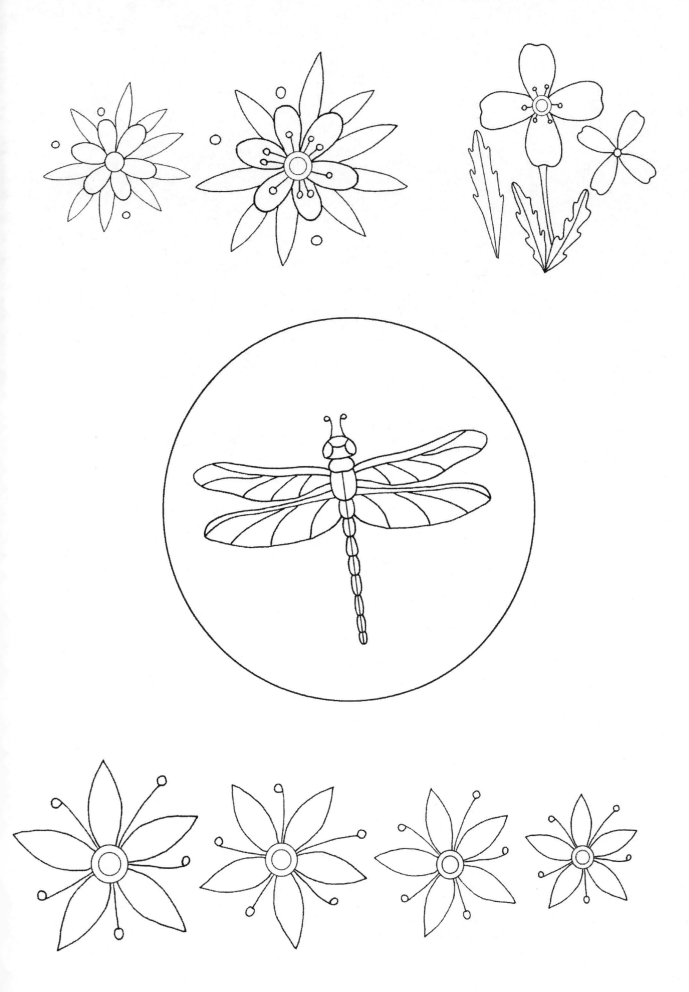

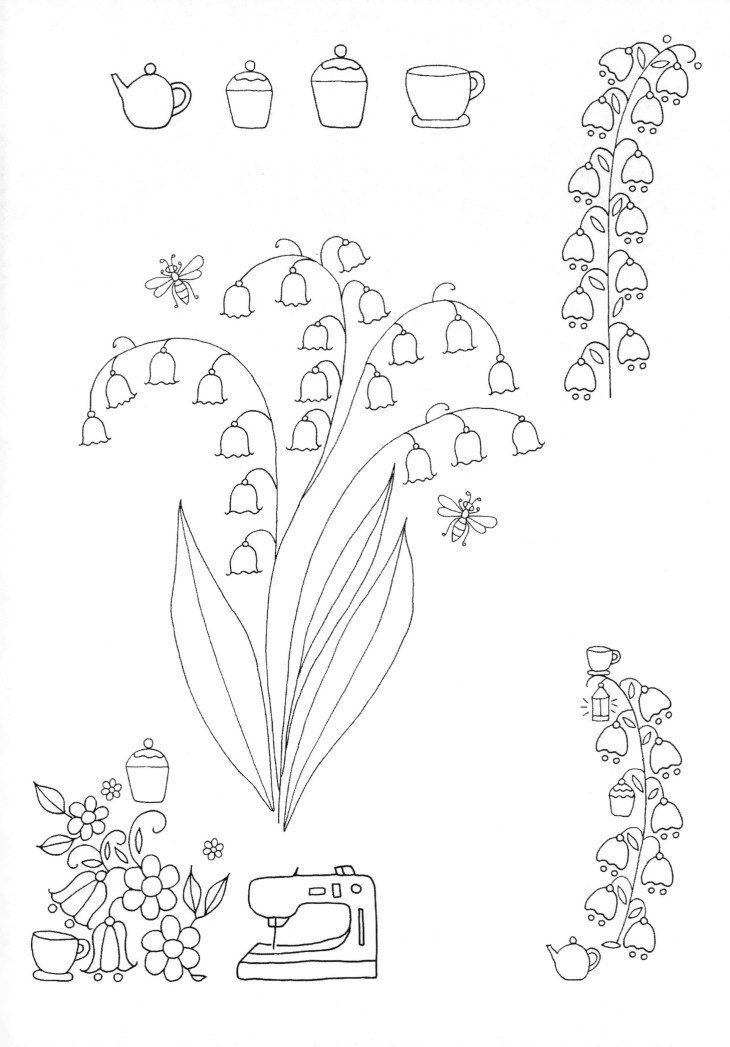

Manufactured by Amazon.ca
Bolton, ON